I0038980

TIME DOES NOT HEAL

STACY–ANN SMITH

ISBN: 978-1-7353610-6-2
Cover Design: Business Startup & Marketing Solutions
LLC

Published by JWG Publishing

Dedication

To my late father and friend Carl Lloyd Anthony
Williams, a fast talker and walker, loving father
and husband, faithful servant of God and His
people; a love that will never die.

Table Of Contents

Acknowledgements

Time Does Not Heal would not have been possible without the gifts that God has given me, the experiences he has taken me through and the strength and courage that he bestowed to overcome them. Lord, you have shown me unconditional love, patience, mercy and favor, for which I will always honor you. All glory and all praise to the Most High God for his loving kindness toward me.

Love and thanks to my children, Daniel and Debra-Kaye Smith, two amazing human beings who have taught me so much about myself. You have been a source of constant inspiration and motivation, and I will forever be grateful to God for choosing me to be your mother.

Love and more love to my family for their constant support, for being cheerleaders, for scraping me up off the floor and holding me up when I didn't have the strength to stand. I will forever be grateful to have you in my life — my mother Beryl (aka Miss Peggy), my sisters Karen and Camille, and my brother Patrick.

Thanks to my publisher Joan Wright Good and the JWG Publishing House team for their expert guidance and professionalism. You are truly amazing!

Finally, I want to acknowledge the value in the lessons life has taught me, the character they have built and the peace and joy that now pass all understanding.

Introduction

Whoever first said 'Time heals all wounds' must never have had a complex bone fracture or a jagged laceration, let alone a deeply emotional and heart-rending experience, the kind that leaves you befuddled, threatens your sanity and predicts a future most hopeless. Only superficial scrapes, nicks and bruises are healed by time alone; and even then, some of those still leave scars. Only the slightest of offences or bruised egos are healed simply with the passage of time; and even then, the memory of an ill-timed joke at your expense can leave lasting impact. Time alone does not heal. It is what you *do* as time passes that determines *whether* you heal and how much healing actually occurs. That is true for physical as well as emotional wounds.

Any medical professional will tell you that a small cut, depending on what inflicted it, can outwardly seem like a simple wound, until subtle signs indicate an infection brewing beneath the surface. Pain, soreness and redness of the skin that is slightly warm to the touch all hint of something more serious. If you're not paying attention, you might even miss the signs until the pain is severe and you have a situation that requires urgent medical intervention. The same is true for emotional hurt that, for one reason or another, we dismiss or try to gloss over until the effects of that hurt begin to manifest in ways that damage our health and our relationships with others. The inability to sleep and concentrate, the refusal to trust, the tendency to be always on the defensive, and a willingness to tolerate gross disrespect all suggest there is something beneath the surface that requires investigation. The truth is, while most of us will readily see physical wounds, we are less likely to pay attention to our emotional and psychological need for healing.

Our readiness to legitimize emotional hurt and the impact that it has on our overall well-being often depends on socialization. As Jamaicans born in the late 1970s in an inner-city community, where the focus of life was often on the basic amenities and eking out a decent living, we were never raised to be concerned about mental health. You were either mad or sane, and no one wanted to be labelled the former for fear of the dreadful stigma that was attached. Community members who were 'not quite right' were whispered about or laughed at, and largely avoided. As inappropriate and unhelpful as that may have been, at least there was acknowledgement of their predicament. We all knew something was wrong, whether we could define it or wanted to do anything about it. But no one ever talked about emotional scars. I can't recall ever hearing relatives or neighbours talk about childhood trauma, death or heartbreak as having long-term emotional consequences that could require intervention. I did not grow up with an appreciation for my own emotional state and the need to monitor, protect or preserve it. In my teens, I saw heartbreak and loss largely as pop culture phenomena, referenced in movies and R&B songs, with little relevance to real life. It was, therefore, no surprise that I had absolutely no idea how to handle emotional wounds or even identify the hurt that I had been carrying. Before I knew it, it had begun to affect my decision-making as a young adult.

If by itself, time heals all wounds, then by the time I turned twenty, I should have been fully recovered from damage to my self-image and self-worth suffered as a child of five and six years old. Fifteen years should have been more than enough time for me to at least begin the process of recovery. But like so many young women who are fed a steady diet of self-doubt and negative notions of who they are, passing time with no active work toward healing only worsened my predicament. It was not until much later in life that I came to truly understand that healing emotional wounds, deep or otherwise, must be intentional. It hardly ever happens by chance or simply with the passage of time.

Of course, some aspects of loss do lessen over time for some people. The pain of losing a loved one, for instance, may never go away completely — but, over time, it is not as sharp or as raw as it was in those first few months. After the first eighteen months, many people coping with the loss of someone close, begin to feel less pain, anger, guilt, regret and other negative emotions associated with the loss. However, there are those who get trapped in their grief and spend years stuck in an emotional space that renders them incapable of functioning optimally. They are held captive in a twilight zone of mourning, self-recriminations and unforgiveness.

As a people, we do not recognize the connection between our emotional state and our ability to be and do. So many talented Jamaicans have never been able to self-actualize, either because of the trauma they experienced as a child, heartbreak they suffered as a young adult or ongoing abusive relationships. A weakened or compromised emotional state can be just as debilitating as a weak immune system, leaving you susceptible to all kinds of 'viruses' that infect your emotions, drain your energy, kill your self-confidence and render your dreams dead-on-arrival. Common emotional 'viruses' include disrespect, hyper-criticism, abuse, rejection, betrayal, negative self-talk and what we Jamaicans call 'bad mind'.

While I am fully aware that emotional well-being is critical for both men and women, and I am definitely interested in greater dialogue around the issue on both sides of the gender divide, I can only speak to personal experiences as a young girl growing up and a more vibrant woman now in the prime of her life. Our lives are so deeply intertwined that it makes perfect sense for us as a collective to learn more about and focus on emotional healing for the men and women in our lives. It hardly helps if I am a well person, but my relatives, coworkers and significant other are all limping along with deep emotional wounds. Their hurt will quickly become my reality.

For now, I can only share my experiences in the hope that it will enlighten, empower and inspire other women to action – whether it is to work on themselves or their relationships with family, children and spouses. I share because I truly believe that there was purpose in my pain, that the hard lessons I have learned can help others navigate the valley experiences of their own lives. It is my fervent wish to use my pain and loss, and my journey to healing, to help others create a roadmap to their own recovery. At this point, I should warn that the healing process is not a clean and tidy exercise. It involves asking and answering some tough questions about yourself. It involves self-discovery. The process of healing starts with knowledge. As my late, great father always said, 'The greatest thing is to know'.

Chapter 1

LESSONS FROM
A CLOTHESPIN

I was born and raised in Kingston, Jamaica. Just about a third of the 2.7 million population live in the capital. I learned as a seventeen-year-old, newly employed in my first real job, that most Kingston residents migrated there from rural communities, eager to find opportunities for a better life. None of my colleagues in that small records office was actually from Kingston. I had no idea that intra-island migration was such a huge phenomenon. In fact, there was a lot that I did not know, growing up as I did with little exposure in the pre-social media era, where the parish library was the repository of all knowledge. You could perhaps say I was sheltered. Indeed, it was not until the second grade, as a seven-year-old, when I learned that it was possible for a child and their mother to have different last names. My parents were married, and all of us were Williams. This was not the lived experience of my best friend, Marsha-Gaye Wilson, whose mom I referred to as Aunty Pat, assuming all the while that she was Patsy Wilson. Imagine my surprise when in class, I noticed that Marsha had written 'Patsy Campbell' on her family tree. I pointed out the error immediately and she quite rightly advised me that her mother and father were not married and so she and Aunty Pat had different last names. I was perplexed. A quick chat with Mommy when she came to pick us up, and the matter was settled. Apparently, you did *not* have to be married to have children.

Looking back, I recognize that those kinds of conversations hardly ever happened in my household. I was more or less oblivious to most things of that nature as a child. Our family lived in Maverley, which in those days of the mid 1980s, had already earned the label of 'ghetto.' While the community could not be described as 'well-to-do,' the Folkes' (my grandparents) were highly respected and did their best to instill in us a sense of pride, especially from my grandfather. Later, I discovered that at the heart of that pride was a heavy dose of arrogance. Mr. Folkes truly believed that he was better and smarter than most people, especially those with darker skin.

Born in 1921, and raised at a time when the vestiges of post-colonial life were still suffocating any hope of mental emancipation, Mr. Folkes believed that his brown skin made him better off than those unfortunate enough to be born darker. He prized himself for his straight nose and 'pretty' hair. Without a doubt, his worldview was framed by the time and space in which he grew up. As a young man in rural Jamaica in the early 1930s, Mr. Folkes lived in a deeply fragmented society where race and color created impenetrable lines of demarcation. Social angst had been intensifying amid worsening economic conditions triggered by the Great Depression, and despite the rise of newly formed political parties and social consciousness, there was hardly any relief for the racism that was still deeply embedded in the Jamaican psyche. It was therefore no surprise that my grandfather believed that white was right, and, for the black man, proximity to the lighter hue was the only hope of salvation. By the time he met my grandmother and began having children in the early 1950s, there was no indication that the teachings of Garvey or any other Pan-Africanist had made an impact on his mindset. To the contrary, Mr. Folkes was known for pejorative utterances confirming his dislike for his dark- skinned neighbors and a distinct preference for 'high color' people.

We called him Daddy Folkes, to make the distinction between him and my father, Carl, who had come to live in the house at Field Road after he married Mr. Folkes' eldest daughter, Peggy. In a big family house where she and two of her adult siblings still lived and called their father 'daddy', we avoided confusion by customizing their titles, creating 'Daddy Folkes' and 'Daddy Carl' for ease of communication. Looking back in the pursuit of healing, I recognize that they had both played the role of father figure for me. They were both strong men, with opinions they were not afraid to share. They were good providers and hard workers. Beyond those qualities, they could not have been more different. The contrasts read like a Dickensian plot twist. Where Daddy Folkes was a belligerent tyrant, Daddy Carl was a servant leader. Daddy Folkes was unkind and mean-spirited, while Daddy Carl was generous and affable. Daddy Folkes was the typical Jamaican man, who rarely meddled in housework or other menial tasks left to the women, while Daddy Carl never hesitated to jump in and get his hands dirty, whether it was cleaning, cooking, laundry or minding his four children, three of whom were girls.

By the time I was three, Daddy Carl had landed a job with a cruise line and headed off to work on the ship for months at a time. With three small children and a wife to support, he jumped at the chance to earn hard currency in the hopes of putting his own roof over our heads. But the job was expensive, the cost of which was borne by us all. Daddy Carl came home a few times each year for vacation, which was not enough to counter the negative influence of Daddy Folkes, who had become our main father figure. My dad's absence was felt. My mother was miserable. She was left at the mercy of her father, who used every opportunity to demonstrate and articulate his disapproval of her, even in the presence of her children. She wanted to move out, but succumbed to the fear of having to manage four small children alone, and buckled under the pressure of my grandmother, who actively discouraged it and consistently planted and watered seeds of doubt. Later as a young adult, I asked Daddy Carl about his decision to work overseas for so many years, and he confessed that being away from his family had been a bad idea which had cost him dearly. For starters, it had contributed to the ruin of his marriage and robbed him of the opportunity to be present in his children's lives. It had also left a void that Daddy Folkes had unwittingly filled.

I knew very early that my grandfather did not like us. He had always had a rocky relationship with my mother, judged my father for his inability to provide a home for us, and seemed terribly put out by me and my siblings, who were the offspring of what he clearly thought was an ill-advised union. He disapproved of my father for many reasons, some of which remain unknown. Dark-skinned Daddy Carl was 'too black', and as my grandfather often said, "Nuttn too black nuh good." Then again, very few persons qualified for his approval. Who knows why he didn't like us. Maybe the inconvenience of having five new souls under his roof when he was hoping to divest himself of my mother was the icing on the cake. Maybe he had harbored hopes of retiring quietly with his wife without a growing number of noisy grandchildren. Who knows. What is for sure is that Daddy Folkes was a cantankerous man who used every opportunity to make life unpleasant for everyone around him. My memories of our interactions are peppered with emotions of fear, pain and anger. Don't get me wrong—

he was not all bad. He did allow us to live under his roof, sometimes rent-free, for several years. He also grudgingly provided financial support when remittances were late. But his tongue was as sharp as a razor and his words cut deep. Long before I knew what it meant, my grandfather was calling people cocksuckers. My grandmother referred to him as a 'bad-wud merchant,' which meant he could curse a blue streak without provocation. He always seemed to be upset about something, and we were convinced he would prowl around the yard looking for reasons to quarrel. He would come and just shut off the TV as we sat watching, declaring that he was paying the electricity bill and owned the couch we were sitting on, so could therefore do as he pleased. As a teenager, I learned that my grandfather was also known for his mendacious tendencies and had bought none of the furniture in the house, nor was he shouldering the utility bills on his own. I do recall attempts by my mother to challenge his claims that my parents were deadbeats, and the uproar that it caused. It was no surprise that she took the less confrontational route of simply ignoring his rants. Like everyone else in his domain, we, the children, were regularly called fools and idiots, and told that we were stupid.

By far the most damaging however, was his practice of putting a clothespin on my nose. As I've already shared, Daddy Folkes was obsessed with his nose and how straight it was. He often commented on other people's noses, using denigrating terms that revealed his negative opinion of blackness. I remember asking my grandfather once why he didn't like black people and if that meant that he didn't like himself. Needless to say, I was quickly reprimanded and threatened with a beating.

That small wooden clothespin did damage that he nor I could ever have imagined, as I sat with my nose in a vice for minutes at a time. The pinching and squeezing of the wood on the area just below the bridge was uncomfortable, but not necessarily painful. I have never asked my mother why she allowed it, because I knew. Daddy Folkes was a bully, and she was afraid to cross him. I struggle to recall how old I was when it started, when he stopped doing it or for how long the devilish contraption would sit on my face. What is undeniable is the lasting impact and the very powerful messages it sent to my still-developing brain. According to that clothespin, my nose was too big and ugly. It was shaped like a black nose, and there was nothing worse than that. The clothespin was the first to identify my imperfections, starting with the one sitting prominently in the middle of my face where the whole world could see it. The clothespin was a weapon wielded by my poor misguided, mean-spirited grandfather; together they taught me to be ashamed of the face that God gave me. I can confidently say this was the beginning of a long struggle with my self-esteem.

Of course, this low estimation of myself was not just because of that wretched clothespin. I grew up in a house where we watched US soap operas like *Falcon Crest* and *Dallas*, in which the representation of female beauty was white and thin. None of the women in my family wore their hair in its natural state. My hair was described as tough, regularly snapping plastic combs with its thickness. Our hair needed to be tamed, and so, by the time I was 11 years old, my mother took me to the beauty salon to have mine straightened. Body image also became an issue as I got to the teen years. Carrying extra weight did not help, especially in the 90s, long before 'thick' was a body goal. I was teased mercilessly as a child. One boy in basic school bullied me relentlessly. At five years old, he pushed me into a barbed wire fence where my arm was impaled for several minutes. The children in primary school were even more ferocious. They would jeer and sing mean songs at lunch break. It felt like they called me every name imaginable, including 'Sour' based on the widely held belief that all fat people smell. I was ashamed, self-conscious and unhappy. Indeed, I was fat and ugly.

Chapter 2

RED FLAGS
AND A HAUNTING
ENTANGLEMENT

Undoing the damage to my self-image was not a straightforward exercise. In fact, the journey to restoring self-esteem and healing was anything but. It would take several more years and an even greater pounding from life before that tipping point, when things began to shift. My self-confidence continued to take a beating long after I had reached adulthood and was no longer under the direct influence of my grandfather. Even after I had started to earn my own money, gone back to school and obtained two degrees, found myself a husband, produced two children, and was actively building a solid professional reputation, even after all that, I was still struggling. The truth is, while on the outside it appeared that my life was on a growth trajectory, I was being reduced every day by feelings of inadequacy and self-doubt, brought on ultimately by the choices that I had made and continued to make. I say choices, because part of my healing involved the recognition that life had not just happened to me. I was not a helpless, hapless victim suffering at the hands of tyrannical, narcissistic men and circumstances beyond my control. Yes, my story does include characters who played a starring role in my emotional spiral, but I was complicit. I was making poor decisions repeatedly, and reaping the whirlwind.

One such poor decision was my pursuit of a relationship with a man who was emotionally unavailable and otherwise taken at a time when I was too immature to recognize it. The relationship, though doomed from the very start, lasted an astonishing 24 years, 19 of those years in marriage. It started in 1995, when I met and fell hopelessly in love with this very young, tall, dark and handsome 22-year-old from rural Jamaica. Like so many others, he had come to Kingston to 'start life'. Mr. Mann was a strong man, assured of his good looks, bolstered by his success with the ladies and full of big dreams for his life. Did I mention that he was tall and handsome? He was also street smart, business savvy, full of potential and knew how to take charge in a crisis. I felt safe with Mr. Mann, who, as I may have mentioned earlier, was very much involved in a serious relationship. I, too, was dating someone else. Mr. Thomas and I had been out a few times and I considered myself his 'girl', though we had never had a real adult conversation that suggested the relationship was an actual thing. In hindsight, it should have been obvious to me that Mr. Thomas, almost twice my age, was also already in a relationship. Inexperience can be brutal.

Being sheltered proved to be an even bigger handicap, a malady from which Mr. Mann did not suffer. In our culture it was and still is normal for girls to be more sheltered than boys, so he would have been more exposed to the 'real world' at an earlier age, with more real-world experiences. Growing up in the 1970s through to the 80s, where misogyny was normalized and hardly ever disguised, Mr. Mann was taught that women were not equal to men. It was, and continues to be, a society where male promiscuity is normalized and even celebrated, so it was not surprising that he yielded to the temptation to pursue a life that was far from chaste. You could definitely say Mr. Mann was a product of his environment.

To his credit, Mr. Mann had been very direct about his girlfriend. However, as many women do, whether they are 18 or 38, I was flattered by his attention; and as my emotions got involved, believed that I was special enough to make him choose me. Again, to be fair to Mr. Mann, he did choose me, eventually – in his own way. We started dating within four months and before long I had convinced myself that I had found my one great love. Here I was getting emotionally tied to a man who had, up to that point, offered me nothing but a good time. He had made no promises and had been careful to mention dates with the girlfriend just in case I had forgotten. Despite his best efforts, I was determined to form an attachment. I recall one tearful conversation several months into our 'relationship' when I declared that I had stopped dating Mr. Thomas (which I had) and was foolishly falling in love with Mr. Mann. The man panicked. He was clearly not prepared for that level of crazy, reminded me that he already had a girlfriend, and quickly drove me home. He did not call me for weeks after that, choosing as he obviously had, and rightly so, to allow things to cool off.

Although Mr. Mann had never indicated a desire or the availability for a serious relationship with me at the time, he displayed what I interpreted as signs of a deeper interest. A little bit of possessiveness here, some attempts to control there, all backed by a powerful expression of his physical appreciation for me. In truth, it was not much at all, but at the time, for a fat, ugly, sheltered inexperienced girl who was unable to tell the difference, it was more than enough. The fact that he was domineering and had issues managing his temper did not tamp down my desire. Nor did his other character flaws, which included a sexist worldview and the constant need for deference from women. His inability to commit in a relationship and be trustworthy need not be mentioned, since those should have been immediately obvious, even to the blind.

Despite the obvious red flags, I continued to pine after Mr. Mann, literally waiting by the landline phone in my family's house to see if he would call. Now of course, my 44-year-old self would have pulled my 19-year-old self aside and given her a stern lecture, but alas, the benefits of hindsight are significant but limited. Sometime early the next year, we connected again, but this time I tried to keep my feelings in check. Dating resumed, on and off again, for months until Mr. Mann announced that another girlfriend who lived in the US was flying in and he would be unavailable for a while. I was devastated. Here I was, playing not second, but third fiddle and it hurt. At the same time, my family was also going through a rough patch. Mommy had been hospitalized with a ruptured cyst and had required emergency surgery. By then, she and Daddy Carl had been separated, and she had been living in an unfortunate common law union unworthy of further mention. I needed a shoulder to cry on. I called Mr. Mann and asked for a ride to the hospital. He came and executed a quick curbside drop off, since his foreign girlfriend was waiting. He could not have cared less about my feelings. It could not have hurt more.

That vulnerability opened the door for an entanglement that would haunt me for decades to come. During what was still an 'on and off' involvement, Mr. Mann introduced me to a friend from his rural hometown who had been visiting from overseas. Mr. Brown called me at the office two days later to 'chat me up,' and at first, based on things he said, I thought maybe Mr. Mann had put him up to it.

I quickly realized that he had not, and that Mr. Brown was actually interested. As unwise as it was, I entertained the calls and gave him my home number, which deepened our folly. We went clubbing before he left Jamaica, and, before long, I had agreed to spend time with him on my next trip to the States. The entanglement was ill-advised, but could really have been listed among the *Stupid Things You Did as a 20-Year-Old* had it not been for another bad decision that I later made. I married Mr. Mann two years after it had ended, and failed to mention the 'Mr. Brown footnote' of my life.

The 'footnote' had lasted for about six months. I ended it just as things started to improve in my relationship with Mr. Mann. After foreign girl went home, something happened and they split up, or so he said. Things with his live-in girlfriend were also tenuous, or so he said, and he was ready to move out and establish a proper relationship with me. I was ecstatic. Things continued to improve — until he announced that live-in girlfriend was pregnant. I thought I would die from the unmovable block of pain in my chest. He begged me not to leave him, promising fervently that their relationship was well and truly over and that, while he wanted the child and would take care of his responsibility, he wanted a relationship with me. Mr. Mann was relentless. I believed him, and we pressed on. The relationship deepened, even to the point of us discussing moving in together, with marriage down the road.

Close to the end of the year, I made another decision. This one still stands as the best decision I have ever made. I walked into Fellowship Tabernacle church and discovered a community that really showed me what the love of God meant. I was hooked. I wanted what they had, and so, in November 1998, I walked to the altar and made a covenant with God. Baptism followed and the inevitable discussion with Mr. Mann around the conflict that had now arisen between our love life and biblical teachings. Being the solutions-oriented man that he was, Mr. Mann simply suggested we move up the timeline for marriage, since all he had been waiting for was greater financial stability. I was ecstatic. We went to pre-marital counselling, planned and executed a relatively small wedding, with family and a few friends in attendance.

Within a few months, Mr. Mann learned about Mr. Brown. Unknown to me, Mr. Brown's sister was a close friend of Mr. Mann's ex. She happily advised him of the entanglement and Mr. Mann took it badly. It hurt him deeply. More significantly, his ego was crushed, and all bets were off. The disrespect was horrifying. I was now at another decision point – leave him, or stay and suffer through what was very bad behavior. I chose the latter. Though I never should have allowed him to use it as a cudgel, the entanglement became like a ghost, haunting our lives at every turn, right to the very end, more than 20 years after it had happened. It became the justification for a series of infidelities, some of which Mr. Mann didn't even bother to hide.

While all that was unfolding, life went on. I had the most gorgeous baby boy in 2001, shortly after which I found the courage to make the decision to separate. After about a year, Mr. Mann came back with promises to change. He claimed to have severed ties with the women in his life and was ready to make another attempt at our marriage. He was not ready, and neither was I. We reunited, but it soon became clear that we would continue in much the same fashion. Another two years passed, and I had the most gorgeous baby girl while Mr. Mann struggled to let go of the past and his natural proclivities. The relationship meandered along, with infidelity, anger and worsening resentment woven into our lives like a strong nylon thread. By the time my daughter was almost two years old, a woman called me at the radio station where I worked to confirm that the inevitable had happened. Mr. Mann was now the father of a fourth child. That sent us into a tailspin. He swore it had been an 'accident' and begged me to stay. We did marriage counselling, and went through all the drama that this kind of intrigue often creates. With all the information that I had at the time, with the overwhelmingly strong evidence to suggest that the relationship was doomed, beyond all reason, I decided to keep going. The next eleven years went as the first six did. We laughed, we fought, we hobbled along in a state of brokenness.

The year I turned 40 was a watershed year, for many reasons. Like many people, as I approached the milestone, I began to assess my life — where I was, what I had accomplished, where I wanted to go. I was not happy with the state of affairs, but unsure of what to do about it. Little did I know that the universe was conspiring to create circumstances that would force my hand. Exactly one month after my 40th birthday, I discovered that Mr. Mann had sired two more children with two different women. Hit with feelings of betrayal, I took the decision to leave our matrimonial home. Mr. Mann begged me to stay. He was relentless, but I was even more so. The next two years were like an emotional roller coaster of epic proportions. Although I had initiated the separation, I was torn between the love that I still felt for my husband and the life I no longer wanted. We went to counselling for what felt like the umpteenth time, but it soon became clear that it was pointless. Despite the fact that the relationship had been a colossal failure, it was a huge part of my life. I had been in some type of relationship with this tall, dark and handsome man since I was 18 years old. My very identity was wrapped up in 'us.' Mr. Mann had been a central character of my story, and despite all the drama, disrespect and devastation, and as outrageous as it may sound, I still cared deeply for him.

Deciding to leave him required great courage and it wasn't a muscle I had exercised often. While I wavered, considered and reconsidered, somewhere in my heart I knew the decision had been made for me. Even if I wanted to, and there were times in those first few months that I did, Mr. Mann had made it impossible for me to stay. My dignity, self-respect, mental well-being and yes, my very sanity, were just too high a price to pay.

Chapter 3

A LOVE THAT NEVER DIES

My father was part of the reason I struggled in my marriage. Daddy Carl was a family man who didn't hesitate to roll up his sleeves and get busy, even if the task was housework. As a child, I remember him doing whatever needed to be done around the house when he was home. He was a chef by profession and sometimes said he preferred to eat someone else's cooking. But every other household chore was fair game. Mr. Mann, on the other hand, was the opposite. He believed in hard work, just not around the house. While I grew up seeing my father do housework, Mr. Mann had not. Again, to be fair to Mr. Mann, he never hid the fact that he didn't possess a domesticated bone in his body. Still, I ignored the verbal declaration, looked past the writing on the wall and expected the man to do what he said he did not like and would not do. My unrealistic expectations were so different from my reality, and I was disappointed. In a conversation, maybe three years into the marriage, I took my father to task for setting such lofty standards. He laughed and encouraged me to talk to my husband and pray about it. Neither worked.

Daddy Carl and I talked often. We were both conversationalists, big on current affairs, loved movies and had many other interests in common. He gave me an appreciation for music and the creative arts. He was a voracious reader and never missed an opportunity for a vigorous debate. The bond we had was rock solid. I respected him as a man, despite his flaws and past mistakes, and yes, he had made quite a few. Chief among his many missteps was the decision he had made to leave his young wife with a passel of children and go off to work in a foreign country, while she struggled to keep us all together in less-than-ideal circumstances. Daddy Carl also had a tendency to nitpick, and it drove my mother crazy. He also had a habit of upbraiding her loudly, in public no less. It's a mystery to me how she never strangled him for it. Suffice it to say their relationship could not survive the distance or my mother's indiscretions. By the time I was seventeen, they separated in dramatic fashion and my siblings and I went back to live at Field Road with my grandparents, while my father went back to his job on the cruise ship.

My teenage years were more or less typical, including the angst that generally characterizes that period and the inevitable clashes with parents. Daddy Carl knew best, and I knew everything. We were both argumentative, very opinionated people who had never encountered a debate we didn't like. My father was a disciplinarian but not in the cruel, sadistic way that I saw demonstrated in my neighbor's yard. He was not opposed to corporal punishment, but it was used largely as a last resort. However, there was that one time when I made the mistake of arguing beyond the point that he considered respectful. It was the day of my high school's annual Christmas Bazaar, the premiere (and sole) event of the year. The planned outfit was a pair of jeans shorts and a top, which, for me, was a huge deal, since it was my very first pair of jeans shorts. In those days we didn't have a lot of clothes, and my father did most of the shopping, which meant my wardrobe consisted of mainly matronly dresses and skirts. I believe it was my aunt who had given me the shorts and to say I was excited to wear them is a gross misrepresentation of the breadth of emotions that courses through my 14-year-old soul. I got dressed and came looking for him to get money to head out for what was already looking like a great outing. He took one look at me in those shorts and told me not to wear them. I couldn't breathe. It took me a second or two to process what he had said and another two seconds to launch into a protest. He listened, then said no. I argued some more, but he would not budge. Panic set in and I believe the decibel level of my voice may have increased. The details of what I said have long faded from my memory, but I will never forget the slap that landed across my face. I was more hurt by the fact that he hit me than by the blow itself. I struggle now to even recall if I had changed and gone to the Bazaar. I only knew that backhand had ruined the day, and left a memory I would never forget.

Then there were the arguments we had when I turned 18, got a job and was fully exercising my freedom as an adult. Daddy Carl was concerned about the clubbing and this fellow who I seemed to be spending more and more time with. He cautioned me about getting in too deep too quickly with Mr. Mann, advice that I happily ignored. As much as he was vocal about my new party lifestyle, he was always quick to praise us when his children did well. Knowing my father was proud of my achievements meant the world to me. He offered congratulations and suggestions on how to go after my dreams. Daddy Carl appreciated the value of education and encouraged us to pursue academics as a means of personal elevation and a vehicle for advancement. He loved to learn, and so did I.

As I grew older, we became closer, having some deep discussions on life and family. He had been almost on the periphery of his own family, having been born as an 'outside child.' His mother, Ms. Ethlyn, had met and had a glorious fling with Mr. Kenrick, who had left shortly thereafter to settle in England. Little did my grandfather know that young Ethlyn was with child, and that she would raise the boy with no connection to his father, not even his last name. Daddy Carl did not meet his dad until he was 16 years old. He shared how Mr. Kenrick wept when he saw him for the first time, and how he embraced young Carl into the family with little care for the sensibilities of his wife and daughter, who were not amused by the turn of events. Their antipathy never waned. They could not, however, dampen the joy both father and son got from their newly formed bond. The day he turned 18, my father went to the national records office in Spanish Town and applied for a deed poll, changing his last name to Williams, discarding Saunders without a second thought.

Family meant everything to him. His children meant everything to him. Daddy Carl never forgot a birthday. Never. That included in-laws, nieces, nephews and grandchildren. He was the kind of father who would call his adult children regularly, just to check on us. His return to Jamaica made communication easier, and we took full advantage of the proximity. By the time he got to his early 50s, he had remarried and relocated to St. Elizabeth with his new bride. She was a good woman who had a great influence on him. I could tell they were happy. His new life involved duties as a deacon in the Brethren Church, and he actively served the community, performing his responsibilities with a dedication that often annoyed his wife, who vigilantly ensured that people didn't take advantage of his natural inclination to help.

What I loved most about my father was his goodness. He always told us to do the right thing, because it was the right thing to do. Daddy Carl was by no means perfect, but he loved God and his family, and was not afraid to show it. It may have been because we both loved to talk and we shared so many common interests, but we talked often. We were on the phone at least twice per week. We talked about current affairs, politics, religion, TV, movies, sports – you name it, we talked about it. In fact, our last conversation was about an item on the nightly TV news. Our justice minister had announced to Parliament that he wanted to remove the Obeah Act from the books. Jamaican laws against obeah have been the source of controversy for decades. Depending on which side of the fence you sit, obeah is a spiritual system steeped in religious traditions from West Africa, or witchcraft and sorcery used to do evil against others. With his strong Christian beliefs, Daddy Carl was incensed at the thought that the Government was even considering decriminalizing it. We discussed the potential spiritual implications and the 'doors' such a move could open. While we spoke, another call came in and I told him I would catch up with him later. "Alright pretty girl," he said, ending the call the same way he closed every conversation. It was the last thing my father said to me.

In less than sixteen hours, he collapsed and died before he could reach the hospital. He and his wife were walking back from their farm with neighbors when his heart stopped. I was devastated. Even now, I can still see him lying there on that cot in the Black River Hospital as the funeral home attendants got ready to take him away. He looked so handsome, so peaceful. His life was over, and mine would never be the same.

Chapter 4

THE TASK
AT HAND

Pain and loss come in many shapes and sizes, wrapped in experiences oftentimes created by an abusive parent, disloyal friend, unfaithful lover, or unjust work environment. Even bad behavior from church leaders can cause real pain and hurt among congregants. Emotional hurt is an equal opportunity devil, no respecter of person, race, gender, religious persuasion or socio-economic status. We have all experienced emotional wounds. How we handle those wounds is as varied as the challenges that gave rise to the hurt in the first place. Through a series of life experiences shared in previous chapters — childhood trauma, a dysfunctional relationship, and the grief of losing a beloved father and friend, I have been dealt my fair share of pain. I know what it feels like to cry yourself to sleep, night after night. I've been at the place where I questioned God and wondered whether he truly cared.

By the time I was 42 years old, I had fully broken off a 20+ year relationship with my husband and was barely beginning to breathe again when my father died and knocked the air right out of me. I had no idea what to do with myself. I barely functioned at work, and if you have had a corporate job, you know there isn't a whole lot of room for extended underperformance, regardless of what precipitated your fall from the leaderboard. I had also recently started a TV talk show, and was only able to keep that afloat because of an amazing group of talented professionals whom God had handpicked for my team. I was drowning, barking at my children all the time, more forgetful than I had ever been. The constant pain in my chest was physical, an ever-present companion. My hair had fallen out, leaving bald spots in the front, my period had disappeared for months at a time and my weight was bouncing like an old truck on a bumpy country road.

The tipping point came as I left the nail salon one Thursday evening in August of 2019. I drove out of the business complex and joined the line of traffic on the busy artery that connected two major thoroughfares. The next thing I knew, I had run into the back of a white Toyota Corolla. I had no idea how it happened. It seems as if my mind had just drifted away and so had my car. Luckily, the damage was negligible, and the driver was kind. It was the wakeup call that I needed. After a brief inspection and decision to handle the damage herself, the concerned driver asked if I was 'ok,' and bid me a good night. I got back into my car and started to talk to God as I drove home. I asked him, as I had done a dozen times before, to give me the grace to pull myself together. I cannot say there was anything special about this prayer, but I do know that I was never more determined to take control of my life. Things could not continue as they were. Here I was with two children at the critical teenage juncture of their lives, still reeling from the impact of the breakup of our family, and their mother barely able to function. Living with me was like trying to navigate a minefield — one minute I was in good spirits, and the next I was snapping like a rabid dog. They needed their mother, and I needed to find some stability in the midst of the chaos that was our life.

The next morning, I called my therapist. Now as I shared earlier, there is a reticence among Jamaicans to seek help for any malady that involves the mind or the emotions. We are a people who, for the most part, will see a doctor for physical ailments. We will even ask for prayer, acknowledging the need for spiritual intervention. However, while some will fork out huge wads of cash to see an 'obeah man' (witch doctor) to 'fix' problems, they are loath to admit they need a trained mental health professional. I have often said few Jamaicans would get a gunshot wound and ignore it, and yet they would rather bleed out emotionally, than seek help for their emotional or mental wellbeing. For many Jamaicans, seeing a counselor or psychologist means you are 'mad,' and to them, there are few things worse than that. Still others believe that admitting you need help is a sign of weakness. Whatever the reason, I am happy to say that thankfully, I was never of that opinion.

In fact, I had been doing counselling sessions on and off for about a year, and while I appreciated the outlet to openly discuss my pain, I wasn't getting anywhere, because I still saw myself as a victim. I was still blaming my husband for all the things he had 'done to me,' and a little annoyed with God for taking my dear father when I needed him the most. When I called Mr. Counselor that blessed Friday morning it was with an open mind and a heart desperate for healing. While I awaited our next appointment date two weeks away, I leaned into my faith and went on a fast, intent on seeking the Lord's guidance on this matter of healing. This is where the heavy lifting began.

Chapter 5

FAITH & FORGIVENESS

"He heals the brokenhearted and binds up their wounds."

Psalm 147:3 (NIV)

After many years of being a Christian, the term 'walking with the Lord' took on new meaning for me. In 2017 when my world had fallen apart and I thought I was going to lose my mind, actually, I was *positive* I was going to lose my mind, I was *absolutely certain* I was well on my way to losing my mind, God said "No Stace, not today." The walls were closing in and it started to feel as if it would be easier just to stay in my bed and waste away. At the lowest points during that time, I felt the presence of the Lord in ways I had not previously experienced. Psalm 46 says the Lord is "a present help in times of trouble" and I proved that over and over during those initial months. He was keeping my head above water, ever so gently pulling me along while I wept and felt sorry for myself. So, when I hit rock bottom that Thursday afternoon in August 2019, I ran to my safe place - the foot of the cross where I had always found love and gentle care.

I cried for more than -thirty of the forty-five-minute commute. It was like releasing a - long-held breath, a world of frustration and heaviness that had been weighing me down. Crying had always been therapeutic for me, though after a while it can become an exercise in self-indulgence if you're not careful. There had been many a time when I had thrown a magnificent pity party, weeping, and wailing and gnashing teeth. Now I look back and imagine how God must have given me side eyes, patiently waiting for me to just breathe and listen to what He was saying in the moment. Whenever I stopped crying for long enough, God would speak. His word came to me in different ways - that still small voice, dreams, and prophetic word from His messengers. He had sent a prophetic word the year before and even as half of that promise was manifesting before my very eyes, I was still nursing emotional wounds that made it difficult to position myself for a greater breakthrough.

Within 24 hours of that tearful prayer on the ride home from the salon, He was speaking again but this time, it was an instruction that I was not eager to follow. I had fallen asleep that Friday night reading the story of King Jehoshaphat for the hundredth time. This chapter - 2 Chronicles 20 - had always given me hope. Faced with certain defeat and possible annihilation, the first thing King Jehoshaphat did was call a fast as his enemies advanced against the people of Judah. In a desperate plea to the Lord, he said, "We don't know what to do but our eyes are on you." This ancient King and I were in the very same position, about to be overtaken with no one else to turn to but God. Around 2:30 Saturday morning, someone woke me up. I heard my name, and I opened my eyes, heart racing, listening for some other indication that there was someone present in the room. I lay there listening for a long time, until my heart rate slowed, and, convinced it had been a dream, my eyes began to drift shut again. Then I sensed the Lord speaking. That still small voice said, "Forgive your husband." My eyes shot open again and this time I sat up in bed. "Forgive your husband," He repeated.

It was not the first time that God had suggested this outrageous feat. Besides the very clear directive in scripture to "forgive those who trespass against us", I had somehow 'encountered' several messages about forgiveness, whether it was a five-year-old sermon preached by Bishop TD Jakes that just happened to end up at the top of my Instagram timeline; or I found myself in conversations about forgiveness and its importance. In truth, I had thought about it, and had acknowledged that it was something I needed to do but couldn't could not fathom when it would happen owing to the current splintered state of my heart. But that Saturday morning, the word of the Lord was very clear. I wrestled with the idea and told the Lord that I didn't know if I could, or how to forgive my husband. "Go and tell him you forgive him," was the response. Now *that* was just outrageous. I was sure that I had not heard right. Go and tell Mr. Mann that I had forgiven him? It would be more than a little disingenuous since I didn't *feel* as if I had forgiven him. But the word of the Lord was clear, and since I had bawled my eyes out, and asked Him for the grace to overcome, the least I could do was obey.

And so as soon as the sun was up, I went in search of Mr. Mann to announce that I had forgiven him. He was a little confused yet cautiously optimistic, thinking immediately that this meant there was now a chance for reconciliation. I explained that getting back together was not on the table and that this mission was strictly out of obedience to God. Whether he believed me at the time or not was insignificant. I had been praying that I would hear the voice of God, I had heard Him, so no matter how uncomfortable it was, I was determined to obey His instructions. I certainly did not feel like I had forgiven my husband, but I trusted God enough to know that if He told me to do something, it was for my good.

For the next few months, I repeated those words, "I forgive him", a few times a day, every day and slowly but surely, I became less and less angry. I cried fewer times each week. I snapped at the children less and my mood became more stable. It did not happen overnight. There were days when I felt like a liar saying "I forgive him" when my heart was breaking, and I wanted to do violence against him. But I tried hard not to feed my feelings. I followed the word of the Lord, even when it felt stupid and impossible, and I wanted to just 'kiss mi teet' and give up on this ridiculous mission to forgive. Sometime early the next year, I realized that it did not hurt to hear my husband's name. It didn't hurt to hear references to his youngest children. I didn't dissolve into a pool of tears at the thought that he might be with another woman, that he might be moving on without me.

The true test, however, came at a family function mid-year when I met his two adorable sons for the first time. Mr. Mann was clearly having a hard time managing the rambunctious duo, and I found myself silently praising God when I realized that I was amused by their shenanigans and not hurt by their presence. If someone had told me a year or two before that I could sit in the same room with them, talk to them and not die of heartbreak, I would have asked if they were crazy. God had done an amazing thing! I had achieved what I will forever describe as a miraculous feat in a relatively short space of time, wholly and solely by the grace of God Almighty! Slowly but surely, He had mended my broken heart and given me beauty for ashes.

In reality, forgiving my husband was more for me than it was for him. Unforgiveness was a burden I was carrying, an imaginary forcefield that was blocking my ability to heal, while opening the door for the enemy to slip in and water the seeds of bitterness. Left untreated unforgiveness can be just as debilitating as a bacterial infection, aggressively attacking your emotional wellbeing and can even lead to physical manifestations. The 2015 book entitled *'Forgiveness and Health'*, details the physical and psychological benefits of forgiveness. The research presented in the text points to the strong link between positive mental health outcomes and forgiveness, including reduced anxiety, depression, major psychiatric disorders as well as fewer physical health symptoms. Studies show that unforgiveness causes 'toxic' anger which leads to poor health and higher mortality rates. Indeed, American author Marianne Williamson was spot on when she said, "unforgiveness is like drinking poison and expecting your enemy to die."

On the journey to healing I also learned that when it comes to unforgiveness, the enemy can be much closer than you think. Mr. Mann wasn't the only person who needed my forgiveness. I also had to learn to forgive *myself* for the mistakes I had made, the poor decisions that had ultimately led me down the path to heartbreak. For years I had been tormented by regret and the belief that I had wasted precious time passively waiting for things to change in my marriage, even in the face of strong evidence that it would not. If beating yourself up had physical consequences, then I would've been wearing a constant black eye. I felt stupid. I felt like a damn fool. I felt like a failure. My Therapist helped me through the process of first accepting what had happened, determining why it had happened, then choosing a healthy perspective that would create a wholesome future. That demanded forgiveness. I accepted that I was fallible and worthy of forgiveness too. Also, knowing that "all things work together for my good" (Romans 8:28) helped to put the events of my life in perspective. Who was I to say that my God-ordered life had gone awry? I embraced the fact that my experiences - good and bad, were all part of my story, and there was immense value in the twists and turns, the mountain top and valley encounters that had fashioned me and set me on a path to purpose.

My journey to forgiveness began with a leap of faith in a God that had always been there for me. Was it easy? Far from it. Did it happen instantly? Of course not. Did it take focus and deliberate action? Most definitely. Was it worth it? Absolutely.

Chapter 6

WISDOM IN COUNSEL

"The way of fools seems right to them, but the wise listen to advice."

Proverbs 12:15 (NIV)

I have said this before, but it bears repeating - healing, the kind required to recover from deep emotional wounds, does not happen by itself. Let me say it a little louder for those in the back - healing requires deliberate, intentional, and consistent effort. It is not an event, but a process. Becoming a whole person after you have been through trauma that breaks you, requires support. At least for me, it did. My issues began in my formative years when unbeknownst to me, I was learning to dislike myself, developing a warped image of my body to the point where I believed that I was ugly. This belief remained stubbornly entrenched in my mind even as people everywhere commented on how beautiful I was. Men, women, children, young, old, black, white, Labourites and Comrades, even people who I know did not particularly like me - everyone agreed that my face was pleasing to behold. Yet, when I looked in the mirror, I didn't see a woman with great bone structure, warm expressive eyes, a perfectly shaped mouth, and a killer smile. I saw a girl that was fat and ugly.

The process to tear down that lie had begun sometime in my 20s. Years after I first encountered Christ, I started to accept that I was really made in the image and likeness of God. My Heavenly Father, Creator of the universe, Lord of all, loved me. Genuinely loved and valued me. Me! That knowledge helped to strip away the lie concerning my physical appearance. I began to see myself as the beautiful woman that I am, growing in confidence. By the time I had left my marriage and began to pursue wholeness, my Therapist gave me a series of assignments designed to first explore why I had believed I was ugly in the first place. I had already made the connection between my grandfather's clothespin and my self-esteem. What I learned at this stage, was *why* it impacted me on such a deep and fundamental level. I recognized that, as the primary father figure growing up, my grandfather's opinion of me was central to what I believed about myself. Daddy Carl had not been completely 'absent' from my life but because he worked overseas for months at a time, for all intents and purposes, Daddy Folkes represented 'father'. That realization was like turning on a light bulb. It led me to a wealth of research around the father-daughter relationship and the lasting impact it can have on the wellbeing of girls and women.

Studies show that young women who reported healthy relationships with their fathers were less likely to become clinically depressed, anxious, or develop eating disorders. Girls who have a good relationship with their father are also less likely to suffer from body dysmorphia, which is defined as a strong belief that you have a defect in your appearance that makes you ugly or deformed. Through the lessons from that clothespin in my formative years, along with other latent messaging as I grew up, I learned that my face was less than appealing. Issues with my weight helped to create an even more unpleasant picture.

During this process of unpacking, I recognized that while my poor self-esteem would have predisposed me to bad decision making and impacted my self-confidence and the courage to extract myself from difficult situations, it didn't fully explain some of my choices. The answer came as I explored literature on Attachment Theory, promulgated by psychoanalyst John Bowlby, and development psychologist Mary Ainsworth. Basically, it says a person's early relationships, especially with parents (or grandparents), greatly inform and impact their romantic relationships later in life. For women, even if you had a bad relationship with your father, you are doomed to go for a similar type of man, thinking you can 'fix it and do a better job this time around. One online reference I found was about a woman who dated only wealthy men as a way of rebelling against her father who had been dirt poor. However, it was later revealed that all the men she had dated were 'distant' and 'dishonest', just like her dad.

In my case, it was not that my husband was exactly like my grandfather. Truthfully, Mr. Mann was nowhere near the tyrant that Daddy Folkes was. But there were a couple of similarities - his bad temper, and the need to control everyone and everything around him. While Mr. Mann had always shown an appreciation for my physical attributes, even when my weight had ballooned outrageously, his other actions showed that he did not value me as a person, just like my grandfather. With the benefit of new insight, I had identified the issue and was now in a position to resolve it with a change in mindset, but the process took time, and a willingness to be open.

I also had to face some hard truths about my role in the demise of my marriage. Among the more glaring were major communication issues that dogged us through to the very end. It was amazing how we could have been together for more than two decades and had somehow been able to skirt issues that needed to be dealt with. Our practice of avoidance was due largely to fear of what the other person would think or how they would react. As a communications practitioner, the irony of the situation did not escape me. I had to accept that I had chosen the easy way out at almost every turn, never giving either of us the benefit of open communication or making a decision to walk away when it became obvious, we were doing more harm than good by staying together.

It's not easy facing yourself and the issues you carry. It's not easy accepting responsibility for your actions or inaction. It is far easier to play the victim. It requires so little effort but yields no worthwhile rewards.

Chapter 7

SURROUNDED
BY LOVE

"A new command I give to you: Love one another. As I have loved you, so you must love one another."

John 13:34 (NIV)

The decision to move out of my matrimonial home remains one of the most difficult things I had ever had to do, surpassed only by the task of burying my father. After having packed most of our things on the weekend, I went downstairs to complete the exercise before the moving truck arrived that Monday morning. I had left the kitchen for last. I opened the cupboards and began pulling out plates and bowls when a wave of deep sadness came over me. It was so powerful I had to sit. I cried almost hysterically for God only knows how long before I reached for the phone and called my sister, Mrs. Walker, who had promised to help with the move. She asked me where I was, and if I was hurt. Then, having determined that I was not in any danger, told me she would be there in a few. By the time she arrived, I was listless, overcome with grief at the death of my life as I knew it, despairing the frightening unknown. Those who know Mrs. Walker will tell you that she is tough as nails, not easily given to fits of crying, a ready set down for those who dare to disrespect. Those who know her will also tell you she is the kindest, most loving, gentlest soul you could ever have the good fortune to meet.

If you need someone to take charge in any situation, Mrs. Walker is always a good candidate, and that morning that's exactly what she did. My sister swooped in and started packing, giving me simple instructions, liaising with the moving truck, and marshaling the relocation exercise like a drill sergeant. It was a most precious demonstration of love when I needed it the most.

I believe it was Daddy Carl who told me for the first time that, contrary to what we had been taught in school, love was a verb and not a noun. In the darkest points of my journey to healing, acts of love and kindness were like a balm to my spirit, soothing and infusing me with the strength to keep moving forward. It was my sister who put up and decorated my Christmas tree that first year, to bring some cheer to our little apartment. In fact, both of my sisters rallied around me in big and small ways, tenderly ministering to my heart. Ms. Williams, my youngest sister, would check on me constantly, keeping close tabs on the kids, especially my son who was in a critical year of high school, sitting external regional exams. Then there was the tremendous support from Ms. Peggy who spent every weekend with me and the kids, a constant companion no matter the destination. My immediate family was an amazing example of loving kindness and patience, even during those couple of years right after the separation when I struggled to decide whether to end the marriage or keep trying. None of them encouraged me to stay or leave my husband. They were just *there* for me.

My small circle of friends were also like towers of strength and love. They called, they took me out for dinner and to parties. They commiserated and cried with me. One of my oldest friends from high school, Ms. Reid, and I were chatting on the phone late one Wednesday night in July 2019, two days before I was scheduled to head cross country to Montego Bay for an annual music festival sponsored by the company I worked for. It was a massive assignment that required a whole lot of precision to execute. As part of the work team, I would be on the ground for the two main show nights which would attract more than 10,000 patrons each night. Mr. Mann would always accompany me to the annual festival. He had stayed in Kingston the year before and I recalled with dread, the many questions from team members who had asked where he was and why he had not come. I recalled how alone I had felt in that hotel room. As I spoke to Ms. Reid, she asked about the upcoming festival and I told her that I was not looking forward to going 'by myself' for the second year in a row. "What you need to do is come with me," I said, with no real expectation that she would leave her home in Florida and fly to Jamaica on such short notice. She paused for a minute and said, "You know what, I'm gonna come." I was blown away. Within 24 hours she had bought her ticket. I picked her up that Friday morning from the Norman Manley International Airport and within a couple of hours, we were on the road heading to the second city. It was a wonderful time of friendship and fellowship. We talked, we laughed, we shared our dreams. Despite the hectic pace of work on the ground, I thoroughly enjoyed what turned out to be one of the biggest and best staging of that reggae festival.

Then there was the love of my church family. Mr. Mann and I had gone to see my pastor at the start of the breakup. Pastor acknowledged that the situation was difficult but said it was not insurmountable. Besides my pastor, only two other church sisters knew what was happening in my life at the time. When my father died in 2019, our pastor and other members of the leadership team rallied around me and my family, praying with and for us, and reaching out with offers of support. I remember talking with the community pastor who was responsible for the St. Catherine area in which I lived. In a large church such as ours, community pastors are assigned to geographical divisions to ensure that all members have access to pastoral care. Our St. Catherine pastor had called to check in, and as we spoke, I mentioned one of the things I would miss most about my father. A deacon in the Brethren Church, Daddy Carl fasted and prayed for his family every Monday. He would intercede for us and pray over whatever we were doing, be it major exams, business ventures, or life's everyday issues. Our St. Catherine pastor took up the challenge and committed to picking up where my father left off. Every Monday, like clockwork, he prayed for me and my family. Since our schedules did not always allow us to connect for prayer, he would record the prayers and send me voice notes every Monday, without fail. That's 96 Mondays and counting.

Indeed, God provided so many great people to support me on my journey to healing, people who may not even have known the impact they were having at the time. Besides blessing me with His word, He sent earthly angels to minister to my heart in ways that I find hard to articulate. And as He did His thing, I did mine, taking full responsibility for my healing and being very deliberate about it. Am I without scars? Of course not. But the scars I bear serve as a reminder of the goodness of God, testament to the power of faith and forgiveness, proof of the healing quality of love.

Chapter 8

A WHOLE NEW WORLD

"I can do all things through Christ who strengthens me."

Philippians 4:13 (NKJV)

While healing had most certainly involved some heavy lifting, took a few years, and a whole lot of introspection and input from loved ones, the results were phenomenal. One immediate benefit was a life-giving boost to my self-confidence and a belief that I was capable of achieving the things about which I had only dared to dream. In fact, there were goals I had not even allowed myself to dream about, let alone pursue. But even before the healing process was truly on in earnest, I began to see changes.

The courage to take the first step to reclaim my power in my personal life spilled over into driving my professional ambitions. I took a creative idea from concept to local television screens and beyond, with a talk show that was syndicated across the Caribbean region within eight months. Fueled by this new 'can-do' mindset, I raised millions in sponsorship dollars for *It's A Woman's World*, commissioned a first-class production team, negotiated deals with national and regional TV channels, and curated content that engaged audiences from a range of socio-economic backgrounds. I had successfully added executive producer and talk show host to my resume at a time when I was still on my way to finding my feet!

Besides creating a platform where we could share the stories of amazing women, empower, and inspire audiences, *It's A Woman's World* helped to renew my faith in myself, and unearthed and solidified a latent desire for entrepreneurship. The show helped me establish my company, Danrak Productions, as a credible production outfit that could contend with the best in the business.

By the time I was making good progress in the process of becoming a 'whole' person, I began to see things differently. My entire worldview was changing. As I embraced healing and forgiveness, I saw fewer obstacles and more possibilities. Healing also meant greater self-awareness and the ability to bounce back faster from setbacks. I began chasing dreams and exploring potential opportunities in areas I would never have considered, never had the courage to pursue.

Interpersonal relationships also benefited from this improved version of myself. I was less irritable, more tolerant, less stressed, and generally a better person to be around. My children commented on the change and encouraged me to work even harder at getting to my goal of emotional wellness. Healing had breathed new life into my very existence, my hopes, and dreams for the future. For the first time, I honestly believed that there were no limitations, except those that I set for myself.

Healing became the 'bread' that was nourishing my mind, my spirit, and my purpose.

Chapter 9

THINGS MY MOTHER NEVER TAUGHT ME

If you know me or have followed me on social media for a while, you know that I am Ms. Peggy's big daughter. I wear the moniker proudly. To know Ms. Peggy is to love her, though, to her inner circle, she can be a frustratingly stubborn human being sometimes. She is kind, loving, devoted to the ones she loves, and if 'loyal' was a person, it would be Ms. Peggy. My friends and schoolmates from primary school remember her vividly as that mother who took us to school and picked us up every day, very active in school life. She was a constant presence. Don't get me wrong. She is not and has never been perfect. Ms. Peggy is and has always been a complex character. Indeed, she is a lesson in contradictions. But hers is a story that I will not tell. Not yet anyway.

I will however share the value I have found in our adult mother-daughter relationship. Having chosen to release feelings of resentment and made the decision to embrace forgiveness many moons ago, we grew closer. I can confidently say Ms. Peggy and I share a comfortable friendship. Although we have spent quite a bit of time talking over the years, there are some topics we have never explored. There are lessons that I have learned along the way that I would rather have learned up front from my mother. It would have been nice if it had been Ms. Peggy who had enlightened my darkness, or revealed to me the complexities and nuances of life, but my mother was never a straight shooter, a say-it-like-it-is kind of woman, nor was she prone to deep existential conversations on the meaning of life.

I therefore had to depend on life to teach me what I needed to know, picking up valuable lessons through experiences that were not always pleasant. The beauty of that kind of 'education' is that it infuses your backbone with steel, your mind with clarity and your heart with love – if you let it. In truth, the lasting impact of your experiences depends largely on how you choose to respond. You have the power to decide whether circumstances alter your makeup for better or worse. You get to choose bitter or better, mayhem or mastery, loss or love.

When it comes down to it, practically speaking, making the right choice often depends on the information you have at the time. As my father always said, 'the greatest thing is to know.' Reflecting on my life, I realize that knowledge or simple awareness could have taken me in a different direction on so many occasions. Of course, there are no guarantees that better information will lead to better decisions, especially when your emotions are in the driver's seat. But, as they say, to be forewarned is to be forearmed. So here are a few lessons I learned along the way that I hope will enlighten, empower and maybe even inspire some of your best decisions.

Love yourself first

'Love your neighbour as you love yourself' (Matthew 22:39) is a command predicated on the presence of self-love. But what if you don't truly love you? How can you show genuine love for others if you do not value yourself or believe that you are worthy of love? Self-love is critical to having healthy relationships and a meaningful life. Loving yourself starts with a belief that you are special, made in the image and likeness of God. Loving yourself means being patient and kind to yourself. There's therefore no room for negative self-talk or destructive behavior. Loving yourself also means acknowledging that you are fallible and will most certainly make mistakes, so a willingness to readily forgive yourself is also important. From a professional or career standpoint, your ability to be and do depends in large part on your self-confidence. Achieving goals and maximizing potential can only happen if you truly believe you're capable.

If you feel as if you are struggling with low self-esteem or self-confidence, start working on it with positive affirmations. Look into the mirror every day and tell that person how amazing they are, how loving, capable and forgivable they

61

are. Write down the character traits you are proud of and goals you have achieved. Spend time thinking about what makes you special and celebrate that.

Now this exercise is not about inflating your ego, because love is not boastful or arrogant (1 Corinthians 13:4). I'm not advocating a puffed-up kind of pride that leads to a superiority complex, makes you take offense at every little thing, or produces a self-centerd world view. Self-love should be about building a good and godly estimation of yourself so you can begin to walk in the purpose for which you were created.

Pay yourself first

One of the major lessons I learned along the way was the value of money management. You could have all the money in the world and be broke in no time at all if you are a poor steward of the resources to which you have been assigned. The ability to make and manage money can have a profound impact on your quality of life. Money decisions are often life-changing decisions. In fact, one bad decision could haunt your family for generations. For this reason, experts agree and advocate for the inclusion of financial education in school curricula, beginning with the value of paying yourself first. This may mean putting aside a little money for a 'rainy day,' or a structured mix of savings and investment involving salary deductions and standing orders. It may even be as simple as being an informal 'partner' with a trusted 'banker.' The amount you save and/or invest depends on your reality, income and appetite for risk. A sensible financial or wealth advisor should be able to provide guidance.

Paying yourself could also involve investments in your personal development. It might mean going back to school, taking a course or learning a skill — something that will give you a return on investment down the road. Training is almost always a good investment, especially if you have taken the time to map your career path, whether you work for a company or yourself.

Building the life you want and maintaining it will depend on the way you manage the resources you have. A healthy appreciation for money and how to use it to advance your purpose should go hand-in-hand with all the other useful skills you aspire to acquire. Financial independence is also important for self-empowerment. Countless people, men and women, find themselves trapped in unfavorable and sometimes compromising positions because they are financially dependent on others. Learning early how to attract, earn and grow your money can go a far way in setting you on a path to independence. Whatever your goals may be, whatever mix of options you choose, never forget to pay yourself first.

Start as you mean to finish

About 20 years ago my sister, Mrs. Walker, and I were having a conversation about relationships and the many reasons marriage can sometimes be so hard. Wise beyond her years at the time, she suggested that a big part of the problem was believing that red flags and issues identified early in the relationship will change over time. "Start as you mean to finish," she said. That truth has stayed with me. I have a friend who often says, "women like SBAs," referencing school-based assessment projects which Caribbean students do as part of their final grades for external examinations. We like to take on men who are 'projects,' in need of work, so we can 'fix' them. For some reason, we see the red flags and somehow believe that things will change, the other person will change, or, worse yet, *we* can change *them*!

Many people marry the hope of what their partner could be, rather than the truth of who they were when they both met. Loving someone involves embracing all of who they are, flaws and all. It's unfair to try to change someone into who you want them to be, rather than accepting them as they are. So, what about growth and development, you ask? Yes, there's definitely a place for that. We are all works in progress, always growing and being shaped by our experiences as we move along the continuum of life. This does not, however, negate the fact that people are who they are until something causes them to *want* to change. Thinking, hoping, dreaming, even praying that someone will change won't get you the results you desire without some action on their part. The late and much beloved poet Maya Angelou said, "When people show you who they are the first time, believe them." Now this is not to say you should not give people enough time to reveal their true selves. Everyone has an off day or two. You just have to pay attention to the clues and listen to what is being said (and what is not being said) long enough to get a true picture.

'Start as you mean to finish' is a philosophy that can also be applied to other types of relationships, including platonic friendships, work relationships and even business partnerships. Get into the habit of showing people how you want to be treated and give constructive feedback. Never be afraid to object when you're treated in ways that do not line up with your values, and be prepared to walk away from interactions and relationships that make you feel less than you believe you deserve.

People reproduce after their own kind

In a sermon focusing on the headship of Christ, maybe 20 years ago, our pastor pointed to the importance of having the right leadership. In his usual charismatic style, he cautioned the single women in the church who were entertaining suitors to ensure that the men they were considering had the right 'head,' meaning that they should have Christ as their guiding source. Without that 'life-giving' source at the top, from a spiritual and natural standpoint, the body, or everything below the head, would be 'dead.' "A man without the headship of Christ is like a headless corpse," he declared. "You can bathe that body, sprinkle it with all kinds of sweet expensive perfumes, but after a while, it *will* begin to stink. You can't take up a 'headless' man then cry when things begin to smell foul." I've never forgotten that metaphor. Now I'm sure that our pastor was not suggesting that only Christian men make good husbands, or that there are no bad Christian husbands, but there's more than enough literature and research on the correlation between values and behavior. There's no discounting the fact that belief drives actions.

What is also unquestioned is the fact that we are the sum total of our experiences, and our experiences inform our decision making and actions, including how we interact with others, run our businesses and raise our children. People reproduce after their own kind, which means you should find out what kind of father or mother your partner is likely to be before you take that step to parenthood together. Happily ever after may be interrupted by angst over parenting styles that could be at polar opposites. Have the conversation around how you plan to raise your children *before* you start having them, and save yourself and those children the stress and heartache of contentious viewpoints.

All things work together for your good

Have you ever been through a season where a worship song or scripture ministered to you in a way that it became almost like an anthem? You add it to your playlist and find yourself singing it every day, and sharing it with friends. In the case of scripture, you memorize it and meditate on the word regularly. I have had a few of those songs and bible verses over the years. There are passages of scripture that have literally kept me sane, given me hope, fed my faith, preserved my peace and given me wings to fly. None, however, has ministered to my heart in as profound a way as the 28th verse of the eighth chapter of the book of Romans. "And we know that in all things God works for the good of those who love Him, who have been called according to His purpose" (NIV).

"We *know*" denotes absolute certainty. "In *all* things", not some or a few. *All* things. "God works for the good of those who love Him," speaks to the never-ending and unconditional love of God for us. It's not a passive, wait-and-see posture. The master of the universe is working all things for my good! It means he remains concerned about my life and though things may blind side *me*, nothing surprises him. And finally, those "called according to His purpose" refers to people who are actively seeking after and walking in God's will for their lives. To love God is to obey his word, to trust and have faith in him. In God's Kingdom, obedience, trust, faith and love are all verbs, evidenced only by action.

One of my favorite demonstrations of Romans 8:28 is the story of Joseph, the son of Jacob, as told in Genesis, who was sold into slavery by his brothers because of jealousy. In the end, Joseph was elevated beyond his wildest dreams in Egypt and became the savior of the very brothers who had first plotted to kill him. What the devil meant for evil, God worked it for Joseph's good. History is replete with stories and characters like Joseph. Take, for example, the late great Nelson Mandela, former President of South Africa. His was a life that exemplified the value of humility in the face of oppression, and the triumph of love over hate and adversity. After spending nearly three decades in prison, suffering the worst atrocities of the Apartheid regime, Mandela rose to the highest political office in his homeland, leading an era of peace and reconciliation that others said was impossible to achieve. What a God!

In my own life, I have seen and continue to see Romans 8:28 play out year after year, time after time. All my experiences throughout childhood, as a young adult, a worker, wife, parent, friend, entrepreneur — all my experiences, good and bad, have helped me to discover my purpose. The darkest times were the most powerful and valuable molders of character. They provided opportunities for me to exercise my faith, taught me humility and forced me to lean on God in ways I otherwise would not have. Without doubt, there is tremendous value in the valley experiences of life. This is probably one of the most important lessons I have learned.

So, as you go through your own journey, be grateful for those hard places. Be open to the lessons life and God are trying to teach you in those moments. Be prepared to put in the work to overcome the challenges, when the time is right. Be patient with yourself. Be loving and kind to yourself. Be responsible for your own healing and aggressively pursue the path to your purpose.

Chapter 10

WRITE THE VISION AND MAKE IT PLAIN: JOURNALING THE JOURNEY

From life coaches, masterclasses and 10-step plans, there are numerous resources on how to achieve goals whether professional or personal, transitional or transformational. Almost all of them include writing down your goals as one of the first steps in the process. Moving from dreaming to achieving requires clear intent, identifying the resources you need, specific plans and the discipline to stick to those plans, especially when the going gets tough. In principle, achieving your goal of emotional healing or improving emotional well-being will not be very different. It starts with an acknowledgement that you are not where you should or would like to be, followed by laying out a path to get you to where you want to be.

Besides the inestimable value to your overall well-being, peace of mind and providing the building blocks for a happy life, the pursuit of emotional healing is a key enabler for every other personal and professional goal. Brokenness is a dream killer. It's often at the root of self-sabotage; and is almost always present wherever self esteem and self confidence issues are found. Naming those issues and finding the best resources for healing should include guidance from a trained professional who can share tried and proven techniques; and provide support. Yes, the journey to healing will take serious work, but the rewards far outweigh the investment. While I cannot offer a prescriptive path to your progress, there are some general guidelines that could get you off to a solid start.

ACTIVITY #1

How would you describe your current emotional state?

Have you ever experienced childhood trauma, heartbreak, loss of a loved one, betrayal from a friend or trusted colleague? If so, describe how it made you feel.

_____

_____

_____

_____

How do you feel now when you think about this experience that caused you pain in the past?

_____

_____

_____

_____

Describe the intensity of your pain (eg. mild, very intense, severe, on a scale from minor cut to bullet wound, I'm at bullet wound, etc.)

_____

_____

_____

_____

Use as many descriptive words as possible to explain how you are feeling now.

_____

_____

_____

_____

ACTIVITY #2

What is your goal for emotional well-being?

I want to stop feeling

_____

_____

_____

_____

_____

I want to start feeling

_____

_____

_____

_____

_____

ACTIVITY #3

What are the benefits of achieving your goal? In a world where you are healed and happy, describe the activities you would be doing, goals you would be pursuing, etc.

_____

_____

_____

_____

_____

_____

_____

_____

_____

ACTIVITY #4

What are your best qualities or strengths, and your most important achievements and accomplishments to date?

Best Qualities/Strengths

_____

_____

_____

_____

_____

Achievements/Accomplishments

_____

_____

_____

_____

_____

ACTIVITY #5

What are the obstacles to achieving your goal of emotional well-being?

1. I don't know how to pursue emotional healing

2. I am not strong enough

3. I'm too far gone, too much has happened to me

4. I'm all alone and there's no one to help me

5. I cannot afford professional help

6. I'm not sure what the obstacles are

7. Other reasons

_____

_____

_____

_____

_____

ACTIVITY #6

What are the tools you believe you need in order to pursue your goal of healing and emotional well-being?

_____

_____

_____

_____

_____

_____

_____

_____

_____

_____

_____

_____

_____

ACTIVITY #7

Write a letter to the person(s) who caused you hurt or pain in the past, outlining how they made you feel and the impact their actions had on you. Include as many details as possible. Be as honest as you can.

_____

_____

_____

_____

_____

_____

_____

_____

_____

_____

_____

_____

_____

ACTIVITY #8

List the persons in your life who you can depend on to support your journey to healing and write things each of them could do to help.

Cheerleader #1

_____

_____

_____

Cheerleader #2

_____

_____

_____

Cheerleader #3

_____

_____

_____

ACTIVITY #9

Create a plan of action for achieving your goal of emotional healing or well-being. Include a list of activities and a timeline for completing each activity. As far as possible, your plans should be specific and include as much detail as you can think of.

_____

_____

_____

_____

_____

_____

_____

_____

_____

_____

_____

_____

ACTIVITY #10

Count your blessings.

What are the things in your life for which you are most grateful?

_____

_____

_____

_____

_____

_____

_____

_____

_____

_____

_____

_____

MILESTONES ON
MY JOURNEY TO HEALING

_____

_____

_____

_____

_____

_____

_____

_____

_____

_____

_____

_____

_____

_____

www.ingramcontent.com/pod-product-compliance
Lightning Source LLC
Chambersburg PA
CBHW072207270326
41930CB00011B/2571